The L...
Easter Island

G000229540

The Last Tree on Easter Island

JARED DIAMOND

PENGUIN BOOKS — GREEN IDEAS

PENGUIN BOOKS

UK | USA | Canada | Ireland | Australia
India | New Zealand | South Africa

Penguin Books is part of the Penguin Random House group of companies
whose addresses can be found at global.penguinrandomhouse.com.

First published in *Collapse: How Societies Choose to Fail or Survive*
by Penguin Books 2006
This extract published in Penguin Books 2021

001

Copyright © Jared Diamond, 2021

Set in 11.5/14pt Dante MT Std
Typeset by Jouve (UK), Milton Keynes
Printed and bound in Great Britain by Clays Ltd, Elcograf S.p.A.

The authorized representative in the EEA is Penguin Random House Ireland,
Morrison Chambers, 32 Nassau Street, Dublin D02 YH68

A CIP catalogue record for this book is available from the British Library

ISBN: 978-0-141-99706-3

www.greenpenguin.co.uk

Penguin Random House is committed to a
sustainable future for our business, our readers
and our planet. This book is made from Forest
Stewardship Council® certified paper.

Contents

Twilight at Easter

The quarry's mysteries

No other site that I have visited made such a ghostly impression on me as Rano Raraku, the quarry on Easter Island where its famous gigantic stone statues were carved. To begin with, the island is the most remote habitable scrap of land in the world. The nearest lands are the coast of Chile 2,300 miles to the east and Polynesia's Pitcairn Islands 1,300 miles to the west (map, pp. 12–13). When I arrived in 2002 by jet plane from Chile, my flight took more than five hours, all spent over the Pacific Ocean stretching endlessly between the horizons, with nothing to see below us except water. By the time, towards sunset, that the small low speck that was Easter Island finally did become dimly visible ahead in the twilight, I had become concerned whether we would succeed in finding the island before nightfall, and whether our plane had enough fuel to return to Chile if we overshot and missed Easter. It is hardly an island that one would expect to have been discovered and settled by any humans before the large swift European sailing ships of recent centuries.

Rano Raraku is an approximately circular volcanic crater about 600 yards in diameter, which I entered by a trail rising steeply up to the crater rim from the low plain outside, and then dropping steeply down again toward the marshy lake on the crater floor. No one lives in the vicinity today. Scattered over both the crater's outer and inner walls are 397 stone statues, representing in a stylized way a long-eared legless human male torso, mostly 15 to 20 feet tall but the largest of them 70 feet tall (taller than the average modern 5-story building), and weighing from 10 up to 270 tons. The remains of a transport road can be discerned passing out of the crater through a notch cut into a low point in its rim, from which three more transport roads about 25 feet wide radiate north, south, and west for up to 9 miles towards Easter's coasts. Scattered along the roads are 97 more statues, as if abandoned in transport from the quarry. Along the coast and occasionally inland are about 300 stone platforms, a third of them formerly supporting or associated with 393 more statues, all of which until a few decades ago were not erect but thrown down, many of them toppled so as to break them deliberately at the neck.

From the crater rim, I could see the nearest and largest platform (called Ahu Tongariki), whose 15 toppled statues the archaeologist Claudio Cristino described to me re-erecting in 1994 by means of a crane capable of lifting 55 tons. Even with that modern machinery, the task proved challenging for Claudio, because Ahu Tongariki's largest statue weighed 88 tons. Yet Easter Island's prehistoric Polynesian population had owned no cranes, no wheels, no machines, no metal tools, no draft animals, and no means other than human muscle power to transport and raise the statues.

The statues remaining at the quarry are in all stages of completion. Some are still attached to the bedrock out of which they were being carved, roughed out but with details of the ears or hands missing. Others are finished, detached, and lying on the crater slopes below the niche where they had been carved, and still others had been erected in the crater. The ghostly impression that the quarry made on me came from my sense of being in a factory, all of whose workers had suddenly quit for mysterious reasons, thrown down their tools, and stomped out, leaving each statue in whatever stage it happened to be at the moment. Littering the ground at the quarry are the stone picks, drills, and hammers with which the statues were being carved. Around each statue still attached to rock is the trench in which the carvers stood. Chipped in the rock wall are stone notches on which the carvers may have hung the gourds that served as their water bottles. Some statues in the crater show signs of having been deliberately broken or defaced, as if by rival groups of carvers vandalizing one another's products. Under one statue was found a human finger bone, possibly the result of carelessness by a member of that statue's transport crew. Who carved the statues, why did they carve them at such effort, how did the carvers transport and raise such huge stone masses, and why did they eventually throw them all down?

Easter's many mysteries were already apparent to its European discoverer, the Dutch explorer Jacob Roggeveen, who spotted the island on Easter Day (April 5, 1722), hence the name that he bestowed and that has remained. As a sailor who had just spent 17 days crossing the Pacific from Chile in three large European ships without any sight of land, Roggeveen asked himself: how had the Polynesians greeting him when he landed on Easter's coast reached such a remote island? We know now that the voyage to Easter from the nearest Polynesian island to the west would have taken at least as many days. Hence Roggeveen and subsequent European visitors were surprised to find that the islanders' only watercraft were small and leaky canoes, no more than 10 feet long, capable of holding only one or at most two people. In Roggeveen's words: 'As concerns their vessels, these are bad and frail as regards use, for their canoes are put together with manifold small planks and light inner timbers, which they cleverly stitched together with very fine twisted threads, made from the above-named field-plant. But as they lacked the knowledge and particularly the materials for caulking and making tight the great number of seams of the canoes, these are accordingly very leaky, for which reason they are compelled to spend half the time in bailing.' How could a band of human colonists plus their crops, chickens, and drinking water have survived a two-and-a-half-week sea journey in such watercraft?

Like all subsequent visitors, including me, Roggeveen was puzzled to understand how the islanders had erected their statues. To quote his journal again, 'The stone images at first caused us to be struck with astonishment, because we could not comprehend how it was possible that these people, who are devoid of heavy thick timber for making any machines, as well as strong ropes, nevertheless had been able to erect such images, which were fully 30 feet high and thick in proportion.' No matter what had been the exact method by which the islanders raised the statues, they needed heavy timber and strong ropes made from big trees, as Roggeveen realized. Yet the Easter Island that he viewed was a wasteland with not a single tree or bush over 10 feet tall: 'We originally, from a further distance, have considered the said Easter Island as sandy, the reason for that is this, that we counted as sand the withered grass, hay, or other scorched and burnt vegetation, because its wasted appearance could give no other impression than of a singular poverty and barrenness.' What had happened to all the former trees that must have stood there?

Organizing the carving, transport, and erection of the statues required a complex populous society living in an environment rich enough to support it. The statues' sheer number and size suggest a population much larger than the estimated one of just a few thousand people encountered by European visitors in the 18th and early 19th centuries: what had happened to the former large population? Carving, transporting, and erecting statues would have called for many specialized workers: how were they all fed, when the Easter Island seen by Roggeveen had no native land animals larger than insects, and no domestic animals except chickens? A complex society is also implied by the scattered distribution of Easter's resources, with its stone quarry near the eastern end, the best stone for making tools in the southwest, the best beach for going out fishing in the northwest, and the best farmland in the south. Extracting and redistributing all of those products would have required a system capable of integrating the island's economy: how could it ever have arisen in that poor barren landscape, and what happened to it?

All those mysteries have spawned volumes of speculation for almost three centuries. Many Europeans were incredulous that Polynesians, 'mere savages,' could have created the statues or the beautifully constructed stone platforms. The Norwegian explorer Thor Heyerdahl, unwilling to attribute such abilities to Polynesians spreading out of Asia across the western Pacific, argued that Easter Island had instead been settled across the eastern Pacific by advanced societies of South American Indians, who in turn must have received civilization across the Atlantic from more advanced societies of the Old World. Heyerdahl's famous *Kon-Tiki* expedition and his other raft voyages aimed to prove the feasibility of such prehistoric transoceanic contacts, and to support connections between ancient Egypt's pyramids, the giant stone architecture of South America's Inca Empire, and Easter's giant stone statues. My own interest in Easter was kindled over 40 years ago by reading Heyerdahl's *Kon-Tiki* account and his romantic interpretation of Easter's history; I thought then that nothing could top that interpretation for excitement. Going further, the Swiss writer Erich von Däniken, a believer in visits to Earth by extraterrestrial astronauts, claimed that Easter's statues were the work of intelligent spacelings who owned ultramodern tools, became stranded on Easter, and were finally rescued.

The explanation of these mysteries that has now emerged attributes statue-carving to the stone picks and other tools demonstrably littering Rano Raraku rather than to hypothetical space implements, and to Easter's known Polynesian inhabitants rather than to Incas or Egyptians. This history is as romantic and exciting as postulated visits by *Kon-Tiki* rafts or extraterrestrials – and much more relevant to events now going on in the modern world. It also proves to be the closest approximation that we have to an ecological disaster unfolding in complete isolation.

Easter's geography and history

Easter is a triangular island consisting entirely of three volcanoes that arose from the sea, in close proximity to each other, at different times within the last million or several million years, and that have been dormant throughout the island's history of human occupation. The oldest volcano, Poike, erupted about 600,000 years ago (perhaps as much as 3,000,000 years ago) and now forms the triangle's southeast corner, while the subsequent eruption of Rano Kau formed the southwest corner. Around 200,000 years ago, the eruption of Terevaka, the youngest volcano centered near the triangle's north corner, released lavas now covering 95% of the island's surface.

Easter's area of 66 square miles and its elevation of 1,670 feet are both modest by Polynesian standards. The island's topography is mostly gentle, without the deep valleys familiar to visitors to the Hawaiian Islands. Except at the steep-sided craters and cinder cones, I found it possible almost anywhere on Easter to walk safely in a straight line to anywhere else nearby, whereas in Hawaii or the Marquesas such a walking path would have quickly taken me over a cliff.

The subtropical location at latitude 27 degrees south – approximately as far south of the equator as Miami and Taipei lie north of the equator – gives Easter a mild climate, while its recent volcanic origins give it fertile soils. By themselves, this combination of blessings should have endowed the island with the makings of a miniature paradise, free from the problems besetting much of the rest of the world. Nevertheless, Easter's geography did pose several challenges to its human colonists. While a subtropical climate is warm by the standards of European and North American winters, it is cool by the standards of mostly tropical Polynesia. All other Polynesian-settled islands except New Zealand, the Chathams, Norfolk, and Rapa lie closer to the equator than does Easter. Hence some tropical crops that are important elsewhere in Polynesia, such as coconuts (introduced to Easter only in modern times), grow poorly on Easter, and the surrounding ocean is too cold for coral reefs that could rise to the surface and their associated fish and shellfish. As Barry Rolett and I found while tramping around on Teravaka and Poike, Easter is a windy place, and that caused problems for ancient farmers and still does today; the wind makes recently introduced breadfruits drop before they are ripe. Easter's isolation meant, among other things, that it is deficient not just in coral-reef fish but in fish generally, of which it has only 127 species compared to more than a thousand fish species on Fiji. All of those geographic factors resulted in fewer food sources for Easter Islanders than for most other Pacific Islanders.

The remaining problem associated with Easter's geography is its rainfall, on the average only about 50 inches per year: seemingly abundant by the standards of Mediterranean Europe and Southern California, but low by Polynesian standards. Compounding the limitations imposed by that modest rainfall, the rain that does fall percolates quickly into Easter's porous volcanic soils. As a consequence, freshwater supplies are limited: just one intermittent stream on

Mt. Teravaka's slopes, dry at the time of my visit; ponds or marshes at the bottoms of three volcanic craters; wells dug down where the water table is near the surface; and freshwater springs bubbling up on the ocean bottom just offshore or between the high-tide and low-tide lines. Nevertheless, Easter Islanders did succeed in getting enough water for drinking, cooking, and growing crops, but it took effort.

Both Heyerdahl and von Däniken brushed aside overwhelming evidence that the Easter Islanders were typical Polynesians derived from Asia rather than from the Americas, and that their culture (including even their statues) also grew out of Polynesian culture. Their language was Polynesian, as Captain Cook had already concluded during his brief visit to Easter in 1774, when a Tahitian man accompanying him was able to converse with the Easter Islanders. Specifically, they spoke an eastern Polynesian dialect related to Hawaiian and Marquesan, and most closely related to the dialect known as Early Mangarevan. Their fishhooks, stone adzes, harpoons, coral files, and other tools were typically Polynesian and especially resembled early Marquesan models. Many of their skulls exhibit a characteristically Polynesian feature known as a 'rocker jaw.' When DNA extracted from 12 skeletons found buried in Easter's stone platforms was analyzed, all 12 samples proved to exhibit a

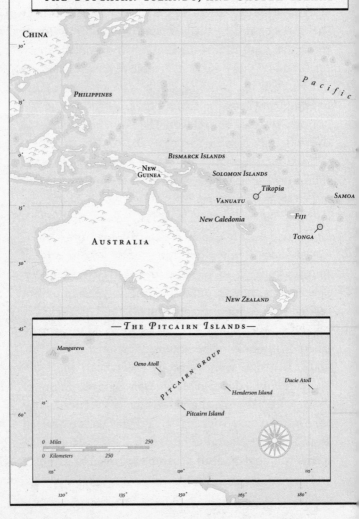

THE PACIFIC OCEAN,
THE PITCAIRN ISLANDS, AND EASTER ISLAND

CHINA

PHILIPPINES

Pacific

BISMARCK ISLANDS

NEW GUINEA

SOLOMON ISLANDS

Tikopia

VANUATU

SAMOA

New Caledonia

FIJI

AUSTRALIA

TONGA

NEW ZEALAND

—THE PITCAIRN ISLANDS—

Mangareva

Oeno Atoll

PITCAIRN GROUP

Ducie Atoll

Henderson Island

Pitcairn Island

0 Miles   250
0 Kilometers   250

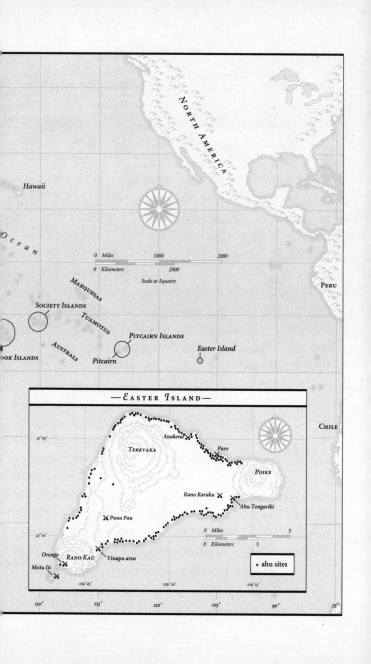

nine-base-pair deletion and three base substitutions present in most Polynesians. Two of those three base substitutions do not occur in Native Americans and thus argue against Heyerdahl's claim that Native Americans contributed to Easter's gene pool. Easter's crops were bananas, taro, sweet potato, sugarcane, and paper mulberry, typical Polynesian crops mostly of Southeast Asian origin. Easter's sole domestic animal, the chicken, was also typically Polynesian and ultimately Asian, as were even the rats that arrived as stowaways in the canoes of the first settlers.

The prehistoric Polynesian expansion was the most dramatic burst of overwater exploration in human prehistory. Until 1200 B.C., the spread of ancient humans from the Asian mainland through Indonesia's islands to Australia and New Guinea had advanced no farther into the Pacific than the Solomon Islands east of New Guinea. Around that time, a seafaring and farming people, apparently originating from the Bismarck Archipelago northeast of New Guinea, and producing ceramics known as Lapita-style pottery, swept nearly a thousand miles across the open oceans east of the Solomons to reach Fiji, Samoa, and Tonga, and to become the ancestors of the Polynesians. While Polynesians lacked compasses and writing and metal tools, they were masters of navigational arts and of sailing canoe technology. Abundant archeological evidence at radiocarbon-dated sites – such as pottery and stone tools, remains of houses and temples, food debris, and human skeletons – testifies to the approximate dates and routes of their expansion. By around A.D. 1200, Polynesians had reached every habitable scrap of land in the vast watery triangle of ocean whose apexes are Hawaii, New Zealand, and Easter Island.

Historians used to assume that all those Polynesian islands were discovered and settled by chance, as a result of canoes full of fishermen happening to get blown off course. It is now clear, however, that both the discoveries and the settlements were meticulously planned. Contrary to what one would expect for accidental drift voyages, much of Polynesia was settled in a west-to-east direction opposite to that of the prevailing winds and currents, which are from east to west. New islands could have been discovered by voyagers sailing upwind on a predetermined bearing into the unknown, or waiting for a temporary reversal of the prevailing winds. Transfers of many species of crops and livestock, from taro to bananas and from pigs to dogs and chickens, prove beyond question that settlement was by well-prepared colonists, carrying products of their homelands deemed essential to the survival of the new colony.

The first expansion wave of Lapita potters ancestral

to Polynesians spread eastwards across the Pacific only as far as Fiji, Samoa, and Tonga, which lie within just a few days' sail of each other. A much wider gap of ocean separates those West Polynesian islands from the islands of East Polynesia: the Cooks, Societies, Marquesas, Australs, Tuamotus, Hawaii, New Zealand, Pitcairn group, and Easter. Only after a 'Long Pause' of about 1,500 years was that gap finally breached – whether because of improvements in Polynesian canoes and navigation, changes in ocean currents, emergence of stepping-stone islets due to a drop in sea level, or just one lucky voyage. Some time around A.D. 600–800 (the exact dates are debated), the Cooks, Societies, and Marquesas, which are the East Polynesian islands most accessible from West Polynesia, were colonized and became in turn the sources of colonists for the remaining islands. With New Zealand's occupation around A.D. 1200, across a huge water gap of at least 2,000 miles, the settlement of the Pacific's habitable islands was at last complete.

By what route was Easter itself, the Polynesian island farthest east, occupied? Winds and currents would probably have ruled out a direct voyage to Easter from the Marquesas, which supported a large population and do seem to have been the immediate source for Hawaii's settlement. Instead, the jumping-off points for the colonization of Easter are more likely to have been Mangareva, Pitcairn, and Henderson, which lie about halfway between the Marquesas and Easter. The similarity between Easter's language and Early Mangarevan, the similarity between a Pitcairn statue and some Easter statues, the resemblances of Easter tool styles to Mangarevan and Pitcairn tool styles, and the correspondence of Easter Island skulls to two Henderson Island skulls even more closely than to Marquesan skulls all suggest use of Mangareva, Pitcairn, and Henderson as stepping-stones. In 1999 the reconstructed Polynesian sailing canoe *Hokule'a* succeeded in reaching Easter from Mangareva after a voyage of 17 days. To us modern landlubbers, it is literally incredible that canoe voyagers sailing east from Mangareva could have had the good luck to hit an island only nine miles wide from north to south after such a long voyage. However, Polynesians knew how to anticipate an island long before land became visible, from the flocks of nesting seabirds that fly out over a radius of a hundred miles from land to forage. Thus, the effective diameter of Easter (originally home to some of the largest seabird colonies in the whole Pacific) would have been a respectable 200 miles to Polynesian canoe-voyagers, rather than a mere nine.

Easter Islanders themselves have a tradition that the leader of the expedition to settle their island was a chief named Hotu Matu'a ('the Great Parent') sailing in one or two large canoes with his wife, six sons, and extended family. (European visitors in the late 1800s and early 1900s recorded many oral traditions from surviving islanders, and those traditions contain much evidently reliable information about life on Easter in the century or so before European arrival, but it is uncertain whether the traditions accurately preserve details about events a thousand years earlier.) The populations of many other Polynesian islands remained in contact with each other through regular interisland two-way voyaging after their initial discovery and settlement. Might that also have been true of Easter, and might other canoes have arrived after Hotu Matu'a? Archeologist Roger Green has suggested that possibility for Easter, on the basis of similarities between some Easter tool styles and the styles of Mangarevan tools at a time several centuries after Easter's settlement. Against that possibility, however, stands Easter's traditional lack of dogs, pigs, and some typical Polynesian crops that one might have expected subsequent voyagers to have brought if those animals and crops had by chance failed to survive in Hotu Matu'a's canoe or had died out soon after his arrival. In addition, finds of numerous tools made of stone whose chemical composition is distinctive for one island, turning up on another island, unequivocally prove interisland voyaging between the Marquesas, Pitcairn, Henderson, Mangareva, and Societies, but no stone of Easter origin has been found on any other island or vice versa. Thus, Easter Islanders may have remained effectively completely isolated at the end of the world, with no contact with outsiders for the thousand years or so separating Hotu Matu'a's arrival from Roggeveen's.

Given that East Polynesia's main islands may have been settled around A.D. 600–800, when was Easter itself occupied? There is considerable uncertainty about the date, as there is for the settlement of the main islands. The published literature on Easter Island often mentions possible evidence for settlement at A.D. 300–400, based especially on calculations of language divergence times by the technique known as glottochronology, and on three radiocarbon dates from charcoal in Ahu Te Peu, in the Poike ditch, and in lake sediments indicative of forest clearance. However, specialists on Easter Island history increasingly question these early dates. Glottochronological calculations are considered suspect, especially when applied to languages with as complicated histories as Easter's (known to us mainly through, and possibly contaminated by, Tahitian and Marquesan informants) and Mangareva's (apparently secondarily modified by later Marquesan arrivals). All three of the early radiocarbon dates were obtained on single samples dated by older methods now superseded, and there is no proof that the charcoal objects dated were actually associated with humans.

Instead, what appear to be the most reliable dates for early occupation of Easter are the radiocarbon dates of A.D. 900 that paleontologist David Steadman and archeologists Claudio Cristino and Patricia Vargas obtained on wood charcoal and on bones of porpoises eaten by people, from the oldest archaeological layers offering evidence of human presence at Easter's Anakena Beach. Anakena is by far the best canoe landing beach on the island, the obvious site at which the first settlers would have based themselves. The dating of the porpoise bones was done by the modern state-of-the-art radiocarbon method known as AMS (accelerator mass spectrometry), and a so-called marine reservoir correction for radiocarbon dating of bones of marine creatures like porpoises was roughly estimated. These dates are likely to be close to the time of first settlement, because they came from archaeological layers containing bones of native land birds that were exterminated very quickly on Easter and many other Pacific islands, and because canoes to hunt porpoises soon became unavailable. Hence the current best estimate of Easter's settlement is somewhat before A.D. 900.

People and food

What did the islanders eat, and how many of them were there?

At the time of European arrival, they subsisted mainly as farmers, growing sweet potatoes, yams, taro, bananas, and sugarcane, plus chickens as their sole domestic animal. Easter's lack of coral reefs or of a lagoon meant that fish and shellfish made a smaller contribution to the diet than on most other Polynesian islands. Seabirds, land birds, and porpoises were available to the first settlers, but we shall see that they declined or disappeared later. The result was a high-carbohydrate diet, exacerbated by the islanders' compensating for Easter's limited sources of fresh water by copiously drinking sugarcane juice. No dentist would be surprised to learn that the islanders ended up with the highest incidence of cavities and tooth decay of any known prehistoric people: many children already had cavities by age 14, and everyone did by their 20s.

Easter's population at its peak has been estimated by methods such as counting the number of house foundations, assuming 5 to 15 people per house, and assuming one-third of identified houses to have been occupied simultaneously, or by estimating the numbers of chiefs and their followers from the numbers of platforms or erected statues. The resulting estimates range from a low of 6,000 to a high of 30,000 people, which works out to an average of 90 to 450 people per square mile. Some of the island's area, such as the Poike Peninsula and the highest elevations, was less suitable for agriculture, so that population densities on the better land would have been somewhat higher, but not much higher because archaeological surveys show that a large fraction of the land surface was utilized.

As usual anywhere in the world when archaeologists debate rival estimates for prehistoric population densities, those preferring the lower estimates refer to the higher estimates as absurdly high, and vice versa. My own opinion is that the higher estimates are more likely to be correct, in part because those estimates are by the archaeologists with the most extensive recent experience of surveying Easter: Claudio Cristino, Patricia Vargas, Edmundo Edwards, Chris Stevenson, and Jo Anne Van Tilburg. In addition, the earliest reliable estimate of Easter's population, 2,000 people, was made by missionaries who took up residence in 1864 just after an epidemic of smallpox had killed off most of the population. And that was after the kidnapping of about 1,500 islanders by Peruvian slave ships in 1862–63, after two previous documented smallpox epidemics dating back to 1836, after the virtual certainty of other undocumented epidemics introduced by regular European visitors from 1770 onwards, and after a steep population crash that began in the 1600s and that we shall discuss below. The same ship that brought the third smallpox epidemic to Easter went on to the Marquesas, where the resulting epidemic is known to have killed seven-eighths of the population. For these reasons it seems to me impossible that the 1864 post-smallpox population of 2,000 people represented the residue of a pre-smallpox, pre-kidnapping, pre-other-epidemic, pre-17th-century-crash population of only 6,000 to 8,000 people. Having seen the evidence for intensive prehistoric agriculture on Easter, I find Claudio's and Edmundo's 'high' estimates of 15,000 or more people unsurprising.

That evidence for agricultural intensification is of several types. One type consists of stone-lined pits 5 to 8 feet in diameter and up to 4 feet deep that were used as composting pits in which to grow crops, and possibly also as vegetable fermentation pits. Another type of evidence is a pair of stone dams built across the bed of the intermittent stream draining the south-eastern slope of Mt. Terevaka, in order to divert water onto broad stone platforms. That water diversion system resembles systems for irrigated taro production elsewhere in Polynesia. Still further evidence for agricultural intensification is numerous stone chicken houses (called *hare moa*), mostly up to 20 feet long (plus a few 70-foot monsters), 10 feet wide, and 6 feet high, with a small entrance near the ground for chickens to run in and out, and with an adjacent yard ringed by a stone wall to prevent the precious chickens from running away or being stolen. If it were not for the fact that Easter's abundant big stone *hare moa* are overshadowed by its even bigger stone platforms and statues, tourists would remember Easter as the island of stone chicken houses. They dominate much of the landscape near the coast, because today the prehistoric stone chicken houses – all 1,233 of them – are much more conspicuous than the prehistoric human houses, which had only stone foundations or patios and no stone walls.

But the most widespread method adopted to increase agricultural output involved various uses of lava rocks studied by archaeologist Chris Stevenson. Large boulders were stacked as windbreaks to protect plants from being dried out by Easter's frequent strong winds. Smaller boulders were piled to create protected aboveground or sunken gardens, for growing bananas and also for starting seedlings to be transplanted after they had grown larger. Extensive areas of ground were partly covered by rocks placed at close intervals on the surface, such that plants could come up between the rocks. Other large areas were modified by so-called 'lithic mulches,' which means partly filling the soil with rocks down to a depth of a foot, either by carrying rocks from nearby outcrops or else by digging down to and breaking up bedrock. Depressions for planting taro were excavated into natural gravel fields. All of these rock windbreaks and gardens involved a huge effort to construct, because they required moving millions or even billions of rocks. As archaeologist Barry Rolett, who has worked in other parts of Polynesia, commented to me when he and I made our first visit to Easter together, 'I have never been to a Polynesian island where people were so desperate, as they were on Easter, that they piled small stones together in a circle to plant a few lousy small taro and protect them against the wind! On the Cook Islands, where they have irrigated taro, people will never stoop to that effort!'

Indeed, why did farmers go to all that effort on Easter? On farms in the northeastern U.S. where I spent my boyhood summers, farmers exerted themselves to carry stones *out* of fields, and would have been horrified at the thought of intentionally bringing stones *into* the fields. What good does it do to have a rocky field?

The answer has to do with Easter's windy, dry, cool

climate that I already described. Rock garden or lithic mulch agriculture was invented independently by farmers in many other dry parts of the world, such as Israel's Negev desert, southwestern U.S. deserts, and dry parts of Peru, China, Roman Italy, and Maori New Zealand. Rocks make the soil moister by covering it, reducing evaporative water loss due to sun and wind, and replacing a hard surface crust of soil that would otherwise promote rain runoff. Rocks damp out diurnal fluctuations in soil temperature by absorbing solar heat during the day and releasing it at night; they protect soil against being eroded by splashing rain droplets; dark rocks on lighter soil warm up the soil by absorbing more solar heat; and rocks may also serve as slow-time-release fertilizer pills (analogous to the slow-time-release vitamin pills that some of us take with breakfast), by containing needed minerals that gradually become leached out into the soil. In modern agricultural experiments in the U.S. Southwest designed to understand why the ancient Anasazi (early Native American farmers there) used lithic mulches, it turned out that the mulches yielded big advantages to farmers. Mulched soils ended up with double the soil moisture content, lower maximum soil temperatures during the day, higher minimum soil temperatures at night, and higher yields for every one of 16 plant species grown – four times higher yields averaged over the 16 species, and 50 times higher yields of the species most benefited by the mulch. Those are enormous advantages.

Chris Stevenson interprets his surveys as documenting the spread of rock-assisted intensive agriculture on Easter. For about the first 500 years of Polynesian occupation, in his view, farmers remained in the lowlands within a few miles of the coast, in order to be closer to freshwater sources and fishing and shellfishing opportunities. The first evidence for rock gardens that he can discern appears around A.D. 1300, in higher-elevation inland areas that have the advantage of higher rainfall than coastal areas but cooler temperatures (mitigated by the use of dark rocks to raise soil temperatures). Much of Easter's interior was converted into rock gardens. Interestingly, it seems clear that farmers themselves didn't live in the interior, because there are remains of only small numbers of commoners' houses there, lacking chicken houses and with only small ovens and garbage piles. Instead, there are scattered elite-type houses, evidently for resident upper-class managers who ran the extensive rock gardens as large-scale plantations (not as individual family gardens) to produce surplus food for the chiefs' labor force, while all the peasants continued to live near the coast and walked back and forth several miles inland each day. Roads five yards wide with stone edges, running between the uplands and the coast, may mark the routes of those daily commutes. Probably the upland plantations did not require year-round effort: the peasants just had to march up and plant taro and other root crops in the spring, then return later in the year for the harvest.

Chiefs, clans and commoners

As elsewhere in Polynesia, traditional Easter Island society was divided into chiefs and commoners. To archeologists today, the difference is obvious from remains of the different houses of the two groups. Chiefs and members of the elite lived in houses termed *hare paenga,* in the shape of a long and slender upside-down canoe, typically around 40 feet long (in one case, 310 feet), not more than 10 feet wide, and curved at the ends. The house's walls and roof (corresponding to the canoe's inverted hull) were of three layers of thatch, but the floor was outlined by neatly cut and fitted foundation stones of basalt. Especially the curved and beveled stones at each end were difficult to make, prized, and stolen back and forth between rival clans. In front of many *hare paenga* was a stone-paved terrace. *Hare paenga* were built in the 200-yard-broad coastal strip, 6 to 10 of them at each major site, immediately inland of the site's platform bearing the statues. In contrast, houses of commoners were relegated to locations farther inland, were smaller, and were associated each with its own chicken house, oven, stone garden circle, and garbage pit – utilitarian structures banned by religious *tapu* from the coastal zone containing the platforms and the beautiful *hare paenga*.

Both oral traditions preserved by the islanders, and archeological surveys, suggest that Easter's land surface was divided into about a dozen (either 11 or 12) territories, each belonging to one clan or lineage group, and each starting from the seacoast and extending inland – as if Easter were a pie cut into a dozen radial wedges. Each territory had its own chief and its own major ceremonial platforms supporting statues. The clans competed peacefully by seeking to outdo each other in building platforms and statues, but eventually their competition took the form of ferocious fighting. That division into radially sliced territories is typical for Polynesian islands elsewhere in the Pacific. What is unusual in that respect about Easter is that, again according to both oral traditions and archeological surveys, those competing clan territories were also integrated religiously, and to some extent economically and politically, under the leadership of one paramount chief. In contrast, on both Mangareva and the larger Marquesan islands each major valley was an independent chiefdom locked in chronic fierce war-fare against other chiefdoms.

What might account for Easter's integration, and how was it detectable archeologically? It turns out that Easter's pie does not consist of a dozen identical slices, but that different territories were endowed with different valuable resources. The most obvious example is that Tongariki territory (called Hotu Iti) contained Rano Raraku crater, the island's only source of the best stone for carving statues, and also a source of moss for caulking canoes. The red stone cylinders on top of some statues all came from Puna Pau quarry in Hanga Poukura territory. Vinapu and Hanga Pouk-ura territories controlled the three major quarries of obsidian, the fine-grained volcanic stone used for making sharp tools, while Vinapu and Tongariki had the best basalt for *hare paenga* slabs. Anakena on the north coast had the two best beaches for launching canoes, while Heki'i, its neighbor on the same coast, had the third best beach. As a result, artifacts associ-ated with fishing have been found mainly on that coast. But those same north-coast territories have the poorest land for agriculture, the best land being along the south and west coasts. Only five of the dozen ter-ritories had extensive areas of interior uplands used for rock-garden plantations. Nesting seabirds eventu-ally became virtually confined to a few offshore islets along the south coast, especially in Vinapu territory. Other resources such as timber, coral for making files, red ochre, and paper mulberry trees (the source of bark pounded into tapa cloth) were also unevenly distributed.

The clearest archeological evidence for some degree of integration among the competing clan territories is that stone statues and their red cylinders, from quarries in the territories of the Tongariki and Hanga Poukura clans respectively, ended up on platforms in all 11 or 12 territories distributed all over the island. Hence the roads to transport the statues and crowns out of those quarries over the island also had to traverse many territories, and a clan living at a distance from the quarries would have needed permission from several intervening clans to transport statues and cylinders across the latter's territories. Obsidian, the best basalt, fish, and other localized resources similarly became distributed all over Easter. At first, that seems only natural to us moderns living in large politically unified countries like the U.S.: we take it for granted that resources from one coast are routinely transported long distances to other coasts, traversing many other states or provinces en route. But we forget how complicated it has usually been throughout history for one territory to negotiate access to another territory's resources. A reason why Easter may thus have become integrated, while large

Marquesan islands never did, is Easter's gentle terrain, contrasting with Marquesan valleys so steepsided that people in adjacent valleys communicated with (or raided) each other mainly by sea rather than overland.

Platforms and statues

We now return to the subject that everyone thinks of first at the mention of Easter Island: its giant stone statues (termed *moai*), and the stone platforms (termed *ahu*) on which they stood. About 300 *ahu* have been identified, of which many were small and lacked *moai*, but about 113 did bear *moai*, and 25 of them were especially large and elaborate. Each of the island's dozen territories had between one and five of those large *ahu*. Most of the statue-bearing *ahu* are on the coast, oriented so that the *ahu* and its statues faced inland over the clan's territory; the statues do not look out to sea.

The *ahu* is a rectangular platform, made not of solid stone but of rubble fill held in place by four stone retaining walls of gray basalt. Some of those walls, especially those of Ahu Vinapu, have beautifully fitted stones reminiscent of Inca architecture and prompting Thor Heyerdahl to seek connections with South

America. However, the fitted walls of Easter *ahu* just have stone facing, not big stone blocks as do Inca walls. Nevertheless, one of Easter's facing slabs still weighs 10 tons, which sounds impressive to us until we compare it with the blocks of up to 361 tons at the Inca fortress of Sacsahuaman. The *ahu* are up to 13 feet high, and many are extended by lateral wings to a width of up to 500 feet. Hence an *ahu*'s total weight – from about 300 tons for a small *ahu*, up to more than 9,000 tons for Ahu Tongariki – dwarfs that of the statues that it supports. We shall return to the significance of this point when we estimate the total effort involved in building Easter's *ahu* and *moai*.

An *ahu*'s rear (seaward) retaining wall is approximately vertical, but the front wall slopes down to a flat rectangular plaza about 160 feet on each side. In back of an *ahu* are crematoria containing the remains of thousands of bodies. In that practice of cremation, Easter was unique in Polynesia, where bodies were otherwise just buried. Today the *ahu* are dark gray, but originally they were a much more colorful white, yellow, and red: the facing slabs were encrusted with white coral, the stone of a freshly cut *moai* was yellow, and the *moai*'s crown and a horizontal band of stone coursing on the front wall of some *ahu* were red.

As for the *moai*, which represent high-ranking ancestors, Jo Anne Van Tilburg has inventoried a total of 887 carved, of which nearly half still remain in Rano Raraku quarry, while most of those transported out of the quarry were erected on *ahu* (between 1 and 15 per *ahu*). All statues on *ahu* were of Rano Raraku tuff, but a few dozen statues elsewhere (the current count is 53) were carved from other types of volcanic stone occurring on the island (variously known as basalt, red scoria, gray scoria, and trachyte). The 'average' erected statue was 13 feet tall and weighed about 10 tons. The tallest ever erected successfully, known as Paro, was 32 feet tall but was slender and weighed 'only' about 75 tons, and was thus exceeded in weight by the 87-ton slightly shorter but bulkier statue on Ahu Tongariki that taxed Claudio Cristino in his efforts to re-erect it with a crane. While islanders successfully transported a statue a few inches taller than Paro to its intended site on Ahu Hanga Te Tenga, it unfortunately fell over during the attempt to erect it. Rano Raraku quarry contains even bigger unfinished statues, including one 70 feet long and weighing about 270 tons. Knowing what we do about Easter Island technology, it seems impossible that the islanders could ever have transported and erected it, and we have to wonder what megalomania possessed its carvers.

To extraterrestrial-enthusiast Erich von Däniken and others, Easter Island's statues and platforms seemed unique and in need of special explanation. Actually, they have many precedents in Polynesia, especially in East Polynesia. Stone platforms called *marae,* used as shrines and often supporting temples, were widespread; three were formerly present on Pitcairn Island, from which the colonists of Easter might have set out. Easter's *ahu* differ from *marae* mainly in being larger and not supporting a temple. The Marquesas and Australs had large stone statues; the Marquesas, Australs, and Pitcairn had statues carved of red scoria, similar to the material used for some Easter statues, while another type of volcanic stone called a tuff (related to Rano Raraku stone) was also used in the Marquesas; Mangareva and Tonga had other stone structures, including on Tonga a well-known big trilithon (a pair of vertical stone pillars supporting a horizontal crosspiece, each pillar weighing about 40 tons); and there were wooden statues on Tahiti and elsewhere. Thus, Easter Island architecture grew out of an existing Polynesian tradition.

We would of course love to know exactly when Easter Islanders erected their first statues, and how styles and dimensions changed with time. Unfortunately, because stone cannot be radiocarbon-dated, we are forced to rely on indirect dating methods, such as radiocarbon-dated charcoal found in *ahu*, a method known as obsidian-hydration dating of cleaved obsidian surfaces, styles of discarded statues (assumed to be early ones), and successive stages of reconstruction deduced for some ahu, including those that have been excavated by archeologists. It seems clear, however, that later statues tended to be taller (though not necessarily heavier), and that the biggest *ahu* underwent multiple rebuildings with time to become larger and more elaborate. The *ahu*-building period seems to have fallen mainly in the years A.D. 1000–1600. These indirectly derived dates have recently gained support from a clever study by J. Warren Beck and his colleagues, who applied radiocarbon dating to the carbon contained in the coral used for files and for the statues' eyes, and contained in the algae whose white nodules decorated the plaza. That direct dating suggests three phases of construction and reconstruction of Ahu Nau Nau at Anakena, the first phase around A.D. 1100 and the last phase ending around 1600. The earliest *ahu* were probably platforms without any statues, like Polynesian *marae* elsewhere. Statues inferred to be early were reused in the walls of later *ahu* and other structures. They tend to be smaller, rounder, and more human than late ones, and to be made of various types of volcanic stone other than Rano Raraku tuff.

Eventually, Easter Islanders settled on the volcanic tuff from Rano Raraku, for the simple reason that it was infinitely superior for carving. The tuff has a hard surface but an ashlike consistency inside and is thus easier to carve than very hard basalt. As compared to red scoria, the tuff is less breakable and lends itself better to polishing and to carving of details. With time, insofar as we can infer relative dates, Rano Raraku statues became larger, more rectangular, more stylized, and almost mass-produced, although each statue is slightly different from others. Paro, the tallest statue ever erected, was also one of the latest.

The increase in statue size with time suggests competition between rival chiefs commissioning the statues to outdo each other. That conclusion also screams from an apparently late feature called a *pukao*: a cylinder of red scoria, weighing up to 12 tons (the weight of Paro's *pukao*), mounted as a separate piece to rest on top of a *moai*'s flat head. (When you read that, just ask yourself: how did islanders without cranes manipulate a 12-ton block so that it balanced on the head of a statue up to 32 feet tall? That is one of the mysteries that drove Erich von Däniken to invoke extraterrestrials. The mundane answer suggested by recent experiments is that the *pukao* and statue were probably erected together.) We don't know for sure what the *pukao* represented; our best guess is a headdress of red birds' feathers prized throughout Polynesia and reserved for chiefs, or else a hat of feathers and tapa cloth. For instance, when a

Spanish exploring expedition reached the Pacific island of Santa Cruz, what really impressed the local people was not Spanish ships, swords, guns, or mirrors, but their red cloth. All *pukao* are of red scoria from a single quarry, Puna Pau, where (just as is true of *moai* at the *moai* workshop on Rano Raraku) I observed unfinished *pukao*, plus finished ones awaiting transport.

We know of not more than a hundred *pukao*, reserved for statues on the biggest and richest *ahu* built late in Easter prehistory. I cannot resist the thought that they were produced as a show of one-upmanship. They seem to proclaim: 'All right, so *you* can erect a statue 30 feet high, but look at me: I can put this 12-ton *pukao* on top of *my* statue; you try to top that, you wimp!' The *pukao* that I saw reminded me of the activities of Hollywood moguls living near my home in Los Angeles, similarly displaying their wealth and power by building ever larger, more elaborate, more ostentatious houses. Tycoon Marvin Davis topped previous moguls with his house of 50,000 square feet, so Aaron Spelling had to top that with a house of 56,000 square feet. All that those moguls' houses lack to make explicit their message of power is a 12-ton red *pukao* on the house's highest tower, raised into position without resort to cranes.

Given the widespread distribution over Polynesia

of platforms and statues, why were Easter Islanders the only ones to go overboard, to make by far the largest investment of societal resources in building them, and to erect the biggest ones? At least four different factors cooperated to produce that outcome. First, Rano Raraku tuff is the best stone in the Pacific for carving: to a sculptor used to struggling with basalt and red scoria, it almost cries out, 'Carve me!' Second, other Pacific island societies on islands within a few days' sail of other islands devoted their energy, resources, and labor to interisland trading, raiding, exploration, colonization, and emigration, but those competing outlets were foreclosed for Easter Islanders by their isolation. While chiefs on other Pacific islands could compete for prestige and status by seeking to outdo each other in those interisland activities, 'The boys on Easter Island didn't have those usual games to play,' as one of my students put it. Third, Easter's gentle terrain and complementary resources in different territories led as we have seen to some integration of the island, thereby letting clans all over the island obtain Rano Raraku stone and go overboard in carving it. If Easter had remained politically fragmented, like the Marquesas, the Tongariki clan in whose territory Rano Raraku lay could have monopolized its stone, or neighboring clans could have barred transport of statues across their territories – as in fact eventually happened. Finally, as we shall see, building platforms and statues required feeding lots of people, a feat made possible by the food surpluses produced by the elite-controlled upland plantations.

Carving, transporting, erecting

How did all those Easter Islanders, lacking cranes, succeed in carving, transporting, and erecting those statues? Of course we don't know for sure, because no European ever saw it being done to write about it. But we can make informed guesses from oral traditions of the islanders themselves (especially about erecting statues), from statues in the quarries at successive stages of completion, and from recent experimental tests of different transport methods.

In Rano Raraku quarry one can see incomplete statues still in the rock face and surrounded by narrow carving canals only about two feet wide. The hand-held basalt picks with which the carvers worked are still at the quarry. The most incomplete statues are nothing more than a block of stone roughly carved out of the rock with the eventual face upwards, and with the back still attached to the underlying cliff below by a long keel of rock. Next to be carved were the head, nose, and ears, followed by the arms, hands, and loincloth. At that stage the keel connecting the statue's back to the cliff was chipped through, and transport of the statue out of its niche began. All statues in the process of being transported still lack the eye sockets, which were evidently not carved until the statue had been transported to the *ahu* and erected there. One of the most remarkable recent discoveries about the statues was made in 1979 by Sonia Haoa and Sergio Rapu Haoa, who found buried near an *ahu* a separate complete eye of white coral with a pupil of red scoria. Subsequently, fragments of other similar eyes were unearthed. When such eyes are inserted into a statue, they create a penetrating, blinding gaze that is awesome to look at. The fact that so few eyes have been recovered suggests that few actually were made, to remain under guard by priests, and to be placed in the sockets only at times of ceremonies.

The still-visible transport roads on which statues were moved from quarries follow contour lines to avoid the extra work of carrying statues up and down hills, and are up to nine miles long for the west-coast *ahu* farthest from Rano Raraku. While the task may strike us as daunting, we know that many other prehistoric peoples transported very heavy stones at Stonehenge, Egypt's pyramids, Teotihuacán, and centers of the Incas and Olmecs, and something can be deduced of the methods in each case. Modern scholars have experimentally tested their various theories of statue transport on Easter by actually moving statues, beginning with Thor Heyerdahl, whose theory was probably wrong because he damaged the tested statue in the process. Subsequent experimenters have variously tried hauling statues either standing or prone, with or without a wooden sled, and on or not on a prepared track of lubricated or unlubricated rollers or else with fixed crossbars. The method most convincing to me is Jo Anne Van Tilburg's suggestion that Easter Islanders modified the so-called canoe ladders that were widespread on Pacific islands for transporting heavy wooden logs, which had to be cut in the forest and shaped there into dugout canoes and then transported to the coast. The 'ladders' consist of a pair of parallel wooden rails joined by fixed wooden crosspieces (not movable rollers) over which the log is dragged. In the New Guinea region I have seen such ladders more than a mile long, extending from the coast hundreds of feet uphill to a forest clearing at which a huge tree was being felled and then hollowed out to make a canoe hull. We know that some of the biggest canoes that the Hawaiians moved over canoe ladders weighed more than an average-size Easter Island *moai*, so the proposed method is plausible.

Jo Anne enlisted modern Easter Islanders to put her theory to a test by building such a canoe ladder, mounting a statue prone on a wooden sled, attaching ropes to the sled, and hauling it over the ladder. She found that 50 to 70 people, working five hours per day and dragging the sled five yards at each pull, could transport an average-sized 12-ton statue nine miles in a week. The key, Jo Anne and the islanders discovered, was for all of those people to synchronize their pulling effort, just as canoe paddlers synchronize their paddling strokes. By extrapolation, transport of even big statues like Paro could have been accomplished by a team of 500 adults, which would have been just within the manpower capabilities of an Easter Island clan of one or two thousand people.

Easter Islanders told Thor Heyerdahl how their ancestors had erected statues on *ahu*. They were indignant that archaeologists had never deigned to ask them, and they erected a statue for him without a crane to prove their point. Much more information has emerged in the course of subsequent experiments on transporting and erecting statues by William Mulloy, Jo Anne Van Tilburg, Claudio Cristino, and others. The islanders began by building a gently sloping ramp of stones from the plaza up to the top of the front of the platform, and pulling the prone statue with its base end forwards up the ramp. Once the base had reached the platform, they levered the statue's head an inch or two upwards with logs, slipped stones under the head to support it in the new position, and continued to lever up the head and thereby to tilt the statue increasingly towards the vertical. That left the *ahu*'s owners with a long ramp of stones, which may then have been dismantled and recycled to create the *ahu*'s lateral wings. The *pukao* was probably erected at the same time as the statue itself, both being mounted together in the same supporting frame.

The most dangerous part of the operation was the final tilting of the statue from a very steep angle to the vertical position, because of the risk that the statue's momentum in that final tilt might carry it beyond the vertical and tip it off the rear of the platform. Evidently to reduce that risk, the carvers designed the statue so that it was not strictly perpendicular to its flat base but just short of perpendicular (e.g., at an angle of about 87 degrees to the base, rather than 90 degrees). In that way, when they had raised the statue to a stable position with the base flat on the platform, the body was still leaning slightly forwards and at no risk of tipping over backwards. They could then slowly and carefully lever up the front edge of the base that final few degrees, slipping stones under the front of the base to stabilize it, until the body was vertical. But tragic accidents could still occur at that last stage, as evidently happened in the attempt to erect at Ahu Hanga Te Tenga a statue even taller than Paro, which ended with its tipping over and breaking.

The whole operation of constructing statues and platforms must have been enormously expensive of food resources for whose accumulation, transport, and delivery the chiefs commissioning the statues must have arranged. Twenty carvers had to be fed for a month, they may also have been paid in food, then a transport crew of 50 to 500 people and a similar erecting crew had to be fed while doing hard physical work and thus requiring more food than usual. There must also have been much feasting for the whole clan owning the *ahu*, and for the clans across whose territories the statue was transported. Archeologists who first tried to calculate the work performed, the calories burned, and hence the food consumed overlooked the fact that the statue itself was the smaller part of the operation: an *ahu* outweighed its statues by a factor of about 20 times, and all that stone for the *ahu* also had to be transported. Jo Anne Van Tilburg and her architect husband Jan, whose business it is to erect large modern buildings in Los Angeles and to calculate the work involved for cranes and elevators, did a rough calculation of the corresponding work on Easter. They concluded that, given the number and size of Easter's *ahu* and *moai*, the work of constructing them added about 25% to the food requirements of Easter's population over the 300 peak years of construction. Those calculations explain Chris Stevenson's recognition that those 300 peak years coincided with the centuries of plantation agriculture in Easter's interior uplands, producing a large food surplus over that available previously.

However, we have glossed over another problem. The statue operation required not only lots of food, but also lots of thick long ropes (made in Polynesia from fibrous tree bark) by which 50 to 500 people could drag statues weighing 10 to 90 tons, and also lots of big strong trees to obtain all the timber needed for the sleds, canoe ladders, and levers. But the Easter Island seen by Roggeveen and subsequent European visitors had very few trees, all of them small and less than 10 feet tall: the most nearly treeless island in all of Polynesia. Where were the trees that provided the required rope and timber?

The vanished forest

Botanical surveys of plants living on Easter within the 20th century have identified only 48 native species, even the biggest of them (the toromiro, up to seven feet tall) hardly worthy of being called a tree, and the rest of them low ferns, grasses, sedges, and shrubs.

However, several methods for recovering remains of vanished plants have shown within the last few decades that, for hundreds of thousands of years before human arrival and still during the early days of human settlement, Easter was not at all a barren wasteland but a subtropical forest of tall trees and woody bushes.

The first such method to yield results was the technique of pollen analysis (palynology), which involves boring out a column of sediment deposited in a swamp or pond. In such a column, provided that it has not been shaken or disturbed, the surface mud must have been deposited most recently, while more deeply buried mud represents more ancient deposits. The actual age of each layer in the deposit can be dated by radiocarbon methods. There remains the incredibly tedious task of examining tens of thousands of pollen grains in the column under a microscope, counting them, and then identifying the plant species producing each grain by comparison with modern pollen from known plant species. For Easter Island the first bleary-eyed scientist to perform that task was the Swedish palynologist Olof Selling, who examined cores collected from the swamps in Rano Raraku's and Rano Kau's craters by Heyerdahl's 1955 expedition. He detected abundant pollen of an unidentified species of palm tree, of which Easter today has no native species.

In 1977 and 1983 John Flenley collected many more

sediment cores and again noticed abundant palm pollen, but by good luck Flenley in 1983 also obtained from Sergio Rapu Haoa some fossil palm nuts that visiting French cave explorers had discovered that year in a lava cave, and he sent them to the world's leading palm expert for identification. The nuts turned out to be very similar to, but slightly larger than, those of the world's largest existing palm tree, the Chilean wine palm, which grows up to 65 feet tall and 3 feet in diameter. Subsequent visitors to Easter have found more evidence of the palm, in the form of casts of its trunks buried in Mt. Terevaka's lava flows a few hundred thousand years ago, and casts of its root bundles proving that the Easter palm's trunk reached diameters exceeding seven feet. It thus dwarfed even the Chilean palm and was (while it existed) the biggest palm in the world.

Chileans prize their palm today for several reasons, and Easter Islanders would have done so as well. As the name implies, the trunk yields a sweet sap that can be fermented to make wine or boiled down to make honey or sugar. The nuts' oily kernels are rated a delicacy. The fronds are ideal for fabricating into house thatching, baskets, mats, and boat sails. And of course the stout trunks would have served to transport and erect *moai*, and perhaps to make rafts.

Flenley and Sarah King recognized pollen of five

other now-extinct trees in the sediment cores. More recently, the French archeologist Catherine Orliac has been sieving out 30,000 fragments of wood burned to charcoal from cores dug into Easter Island ovens and garbage heaps. With a heroism matching that of Selling, Flenley, and King, she has compared 2,300 of those carbonized wood fragments to wood samples of plants still existing today elsewhere in Polynesia. In that way she has identified about 16 other plant species, most of them trees related to or the same as tree species still widespread in East Polynesia, that formerly grew on Easter Island as well. Thus, Easter used to support a diverse forest.

Many of those 21 vanished species besides the palm would have been valuable to the islanders. Two of the tallest trees, *Alphitonia* cf. *zizyphoides* and *Elaeocarpus* cf. *rarotongensis* (up to 100 and 50 feet tall respectively), are used elsewhere in Polynesia for making canoes and would have been much better suited to that purpose than was the palm. Polynesians everywhere make rope from the bark of the hauhau, *Triumfetta semitriloba*, and that was presumably how Easter Islanders dragged their statues. Bark of the paper mulberry *Broussonetia papyrifera* is beaten into tapa cloth; *Psydrax odorata* has a flexible straight trunk suited for making harpoons and outriggers; the Malay apple *Syzygium malaccense* bears an edible fruit; the oceanic rose-wood *Thespesia populanea* and at least eight other species have hardwood suitable for carving and construction; toromiro yields an excellent wood for fires, like acacia and mesquite; and the fact that Orliac recovered all of those species as burnt fragments from fires proves that they too were used for firewood.

The person who pored through 6,433 bones of birds and other vertebrates from early middens at Anakena Beach, probably the site of the first human landing and first settlement on Easter, was zooarcheologist David Steadman. As an ornithologist myself, I bow in awe before Dave's identification skills and tolerance of eye strain: whereas I wouldn't know how to tell a robin's bone from a dove's or even from a rat's, Dave has learned how to distinguish even the bones of a dozen closely related petrel species from each other. He thereby proved that Easter, which today supports not a single species of native land bird, was formerly home to at least six of them, including one species of heron, two chicken-like rails, two parrots, and a barn owl. More impressive was Easter's prodigious total of at least 25 nesting seabird species, making it formerly the richest breeding site in all of Polynesia and probably in the whole Pacific. They included albatross, boobies, frigatebirds, fulmars, petrels, prions, shearwaters, storm-petrels, terns, and tropicbirds, attracted by Easter's remote location and complete lack of predators that made it an ideal safe haven as a breeding site – until humans arrived. Dave also recovered a few bones of seals, which breed today on the Galápagos Islands and the Juan Fernández Islands to the east of Easter, but it is uncertain whether those few seal bones on Easter similarly came from former breeding colonies or just vagrant individuals.

The Anakena excavations that yielded those bird and seal bones tell us much about the diet and lifestyle of Easter's first human settlers. Out of those 6,433 vertebrate bones identified in their middens, the most frequent ones, accounting for more than one-third of the total, proved to belong to the largest animal available to Easter Islanders: the Common Dolphin, a porpoise weighing up to 165 pounds. That's astonishing: nowhere else in Polynesia do porpoises account for even as much as 1% of the bones in middens. The Common Dolphin generally lives out to sea, hence it could not have been hunted by line-fishing or spear-fishing from shore. Instead, it must have been harpooned far offshore, in big seaworthy canoes built from the tall trees identified by Catherine Orliac.

Fish bones also occur in the middens but account there for only 23% of all bones, whereas elsewhere in Polynesia they were the main food (90% or more of all the bones). That low contribution of fish to Easter diets was because of its rugged coastline and steep drop-offs of the ocean bottom, so that there are few places to catch fish by net or handline in shallow water. For the same reason the Easter diet was low in molluscs and sea urchins. To compensate, there were those abundant seabirds plus the land birds. Bird stew would have been seasoned with meat from large numbers of rats, which reached Easter as stowaways in the canoes of the Polynesian colonists. Easter is the sole known Polynesian island at whose archeological sites rat bones outnumber fish bones. In case you're squeamish and consider rats inedible, I still recall, from my years of living in England in the late 1950s, recipes for creamed laboratory rat that my British biologist friends who kept them for experiments also used to supplement their diet during their years of wartime food rationing.

Porpoises, fish, shellfish, birds, and rats did not exhaust the list of meat sources available to Easter's first settlers. I already mentioned a few seal records, and other bones testify to the occasional availability of sea turtles and perhaps of large lizards. All those delicacies were cooked over firewood that can be identified as having come from Easter's subsequently vanished forests.

Comparison of those early garbage deposits with late prehistoric ones or with conditions on modern Easter reveals big changes in those initially bountiful food sources. Porpoises, and open-ocean fish like tuna, virtually disappeared from the islanders' diet, for reasons to be mentioned below. The fish that continued to be caught were mainly inshore species. Land birds disappeared completely from the diet, for the simple reason that every species became extinct from some combination of overhunting, deforestation, and predation by rats. It was the worst catastrophe to befall Pacific island birds, surpassing even the record on New Zealand and Hawaii, where to be sure the moas and flightless geese and other species became extinct but many other species managed to survive. No Pacific island other than Easter ended up without any native land birds. Of the 25 or more formerly breeding seabirds, overharvesting and rat predation brought the result that 24 no longer breed on Easter itself, about 9 are now confined to breeding in modest numbers on a few rocky islets off Easter's coasts, and 15 have been eliminated on those islets as well. Even shellfish were overexploited, so that people ended up eating fewer of the esteemed large cowries and more of the second-choice smaller black snails, and the sizes of both cowry and snail shells in the middens decreased with time because of preferential overharvesting of larger individuals.

The giant palm, and all the other now-extinct trees identified by Catherine Orliac, John Flenley, and Sarah

King, disappeared for half a dozen reasons that we can document or infer. Orliac's charcoal samples from ovens prove directly that trees were being burned for firewood. They were also being burned to cremate bodies: Easter crematoria contain remains of thousands of bodies and huge amounts of human bone ash, implying massive fuel consumption for the purposes of cremation. Trees were being cleared for gardens, because most of Easter's land surface except at the highest elevations ended up being used to grow crops. From the early midden abundance of bones of open-ocean porpoises and tuna, we infer that big trees like *Alphitonia* and *Elaeocarpus* were being felled to make seaworthy canoes; the frail, leaky little watercraft seen by Roggeveen would not have served for harpooning platforms or venturing far out to sea. We infer that trees furnished timber and rope for transporting and erecting statues, and undoubtedly for a multitude of other purposes. The rats introduced accidentally as stowaways 'used' the palm tree and doubtless other trees for their own purposes: every Easter palm nut that has been recovered shows tooth marks from rats gnawing on it and would have been incapable of germinating.

Deforestation must have begun some time after human arrival by A.D. 900, and must have been completed by 1722, when Roggeveen arrived and saw no trees over 10 feet tall. Can we specify more closely when, between those dates of 900 and 1722, deforestation occurred? There are five types of evidence to guide us. Most radiocarbon dates on the palm nuts themselves are before 1500, suggesting that the palm became rare or extinct thereafter. On the Poike Peninsula, which has Easter's most infertile soils and hence was probably deforested first, the palms disappeared by around 1400, and charcoal from forest clearance disappeared around 1440 although later signs of agriculture attest to continued human presence there. Orliac's radiocarbon-dated charcoal samples from ovens and garbage pits show wood charcoal being replaced by herb and grass fuels after 1640, even at elite houses that might have claimed the last precious trees after none was left for the peasants. Flenley's pollen cores show the disappearance of palm, tree daisy, toromiro, and shrub pollen, and their replacement by grass and herb pollen, between 900 and 1300, but radiocarbon dates on sediment cores are a less direct clock for deforestation than are direct dates on the palms and their nuts. Finally, the upland plantations that Chris Stevenson studied, and whose operation may have paralleled the period of maximum timber and rope use for statues, were maintained from the early 1400s to the 1600s. All this suggests that forest clearance began soon after human arrival, reached its peak around 1400, and was virtually complete by dates that varied locally between the early 1400s and the 1600s.

Consequences for society

The overall picture for Easter is the most extreme example of forest destruction in the Pacific, and among the most extreme in the world: the whole forest gone, and all of its tree species extinct. Immediate consequences for the islanders were losses of raw materials, losses of wild-caught foods, and decreased crop yields.

Raw materials lost or else available only in greatly decreased amounts consisted of everything made from native plants and birds, including wood, rope, bark to manufacture bark cloth, and feathers. Lack of large timber and rope brought an end to the transport and erection of statues, and also to the construction of seagoing canoes. When five of Easter's little two-man leaky canoes paddled out to trade with a French ship anchored off Easter in 1838, its captain reported, 'All the natives repeated often and excitedly the word *miru* and became impatient because they saw that we did not understand it: this word is the name of the timber used by Polynesians to make their canoes. This was what they wanted most, and they used every means to make us understand this . . .' The name 'Terevaka' for Easter's largest and highest mountain means 'place to get canoes': before its slopes were stripped of their trees to convert them to plantations, they were used for timber, and they are still littered with the stone drills, scrapers, knives, chisels, and other woodworking and canoe-building tools from that period. Lack of large timber also meant that people were without wood for fuel to keep themselves warm during Easter's winter nights of wind and driving rain at a temperature of 50 degrees Fahrenheit. Instead, after 1650 Easter's inhabitants were reduced to burning herbs, grasses, and sugarcane scraps and other crop wastes for fuel. There would have been fierce competition for the remaining woody shrubs, among people trying to obtain thatching and small pieces of wood for houses, implements, and bark cloth. Even funeral practices had to be changed: cremation, which had required burning much wood per body, became impractical and yielded to mummification and bone burials.

Most sources of wild food were lost. Without sea-going canoes, bones of porpoises, which had been the islanders' principal meat during the first centuries, virtually disappeared from middens by 1500, as did tuna and pelagic fish. Midden numbers of fishhooks and fish bones in general also declined, leaving mainly just fish species that could be caught in shallow water or from the shore. Land birds disappeared completely, and seabirds were reduced to relict populations of one-third of Easter's original species, confined to breeding on a few offshore islets. Palm nuts, Malay apples, and all other wild fruits dropped out of the diet. The shellfish consumed became smaller species and smaller and many fewer individuals. The only wild food source whose availability remained unchanged was rats.

In addition to those drastic decreases in wild food sources, crop yields also decreased, for several reasons. Deforestation led locally to soil erosion by rain and wind, as shown by huge increases in the quantities of soil-derived metal ions carried into Flenley's swamp sediment cores. For example, excavations on the Poike Peninsula show that crops were initially grown there interspersed with palm trees left standing, so that their crowns could shade and protect the soil and crops against hot sun, evaporation, wind, and direct rain impacts. Clearance of the palms led to massive erosion that buried *ahu* and buildings downhill with soil, and that forced the abandonment of Poike's fields around 1400. Once grassland had established itself on Poike, farming was resumed there around 1500, to be abandoned again a century later in a second wave of erosion. Other damages to soil that resulted from deforestation

and reduced crop yields included desiccation and nutri-
ent leaching. Farmers found themselves without most
of the wild plant leaves, fruit, and twigs that they had
been using as compost.

Those were the immediate consequences of deforestation and other human environmental impacts.
The further consequences start with starvation, a
population crash, and a descent into cannibalism. Surviving islanders' accounts of starvation are graphically
confirmed by the proliferation of little statues called
moai kavakava, depicting starving people with hollow
cheeks and protruding ribs. Captain Cook in 1774
described the islanders as 'small, lean, timid, and mis-
erable.' Numbers of house sites in the coastal lowlands,
where almost everybody lived, declined by 70% from
peak values around 1400–1600 to the 1700s, suggesting
a corresponding decline in numbers of people. In
place of their former sources of wild meat, islanders
turned to the largest hitherto unused source available
to them: humans, whose bones became common not
only in proper burials but also (cracked to extract the
marrow) in late Easter Island garbage heaps. Oral traditions of the islanders are obsessed with cannibalism;
the most inflammatory taunt that could be snarled at
an enemy was 'The flesh of your mother sticks between
my teeth.'

Easter's chiefs and priests had previously justified

their elite status by claiming relationship to the gods, and by promising to deliver prosperity and bountiful harvests. They buttressed that ideology by monumental architecture and ceremonies designed to impress the masses, and made possible by food surpluses extracted from the masses. As their promises were being proved increasingly hollow, the power of the chiefs and priests was overthrown around 1680 by military leaders called *matatoa*, and Easter's formerly complexly integrated society collapsed in an epidemic of civil war. The obsidian spear-points (termed *mata'a*) from that era of fighting still littered Easter in modern times. Commoners now built their huts in the coastal zone, which had been previously reserved for the residences *(hare paenga)* of the elite. For safety, many people turned to living in caves that were enlarged by excavation and whose entrances were partly sealed to create a narrow tunnel for easier defense. Food remains, bone sewing needles, woodworking implements, and tools for repairing tapa cloth make clear that the caves were being occupied on a long-term basis, not just as temporary hiding places.

What had failed, in the twilight of Easter's Polynesian society, was not only the old political ideology but also the old religion, which became discarded along with the chiefs' power. Oral traditions record that the last *ahu* and *moai* were erected around 1620, and that Paro (the tallest statue) was among the last. The upland plantations whose elite-commandeered production fed the statue teams were progressively abandoned between 1600 and 1680. That the sizes of statues had been increasing may reflect not only rival chiefs vying to outdo each other, but also more urgent appeals to ancestors necessitated by the growing environmental crisis. Around 1680, at the time of the military coup, rival clans switched from erecting increasingly large statues to throwing down one another's statues by toppling a statue forwards onto a slab placed so that the statue would fall on the slab and break. Thus, the collapse of Easter society followed swiftly upon the society's reaching its peak of population, monument construction, and environmental impact.

We don't know how far the toppling had proceeded at the time of the first European visits, because Roggeveen in 1722 landed only briefly at a single site, and González's Spanish expedition of 1770 wrote nothing about their visit except in the ship's log. The first semi-adequate European description was by Captain Cook in 1774, who remained for four days, sent a detachment to reconnoiter inland, and had the advantage of bringing a Tahitian whose Polynesian language was sufficiently similar to that of Easter Islanders that he could converse with them. Cook commented on seeing statues that had been thrown down, as well as others still erect. The last European mention of an erect statue was in 1838; none was reported as standing in 1868. Traditions relate that the final statue to be toppled (around 1840) was Paro, supposedly erected by a woman in honor of her husband, and thrown down by enemies of her family so as to break Paro at mid-body.

Ahu themselves were desecrated by pulling out some of the fine slabs in order to construct garden walls (*manavai*) next to the *ahu*, and by using other slabs to create burial chambers in which to place dead bodies. As a result, today the *ahu* that have not been restored (i.e., most of them) look at first sight like mere piles of boulders. As Jo Anne Van Tilburg, Claudio Cristino, Sonia Haoa, Barry Rolett, and I drove around Easter, saw *ahu* after *ahu* as a rubble pile with its broken statues, reflected on the enormous effort that had been devoted for centuries to constructing the *ahu* and to carving and transporting and erecting the *moai*, and then remembered that it was the islanders themselves who had destroyed their own ancestors' work, we were filled with an overwhelming sense of tragedy.

Easter Islanders' toppling of their ancestral *moai* reminds me of Russians and Romanians toppling the statues of Stalin and Ceauşescu when the Communist governments of those countries collapsed. The islanders must have been filled with pent-up anger at their leaders for a long time, as we know that Russians and Romanians were. I wonder how many of the statues were thrown down one by one at intervals, by particular enemies of a statue's owner, as described for Paro; and how many were instead destroyed in a quickly spreading paroxysm of anger and disillusionment, as took place at the end of communism. I'm also reminded of a cultural tragedy and rejection of religion described to me in 1965 at a New Guinea highland village called Bomai, where the Christian missionary assigned to Bomai boasted to me with pride how one day he had called upon his new converts to collect their 'pagan artifacts' (i.e., their cultural and artistic heritage) at the airstrip and burn them – and how they obeyed. Perhaps Easter Island's *matatoa* issued a similar summons to their own followers.

I don't want to portray social developments on Easter after 1680 as wholly negative and destructive. The survivors adapted as best they could, both in their subsistence and in their religion. Not only cannibalism but also chicken houses underwent explosive growth after 1650; chickens had accounted for less than 0.1% of the animal bones in the oldest middens that David Steadman, Patricia Vargas, and Claudio Cristino excavated at Anakena. The *matatoa* justified their military coup by adopting a religious cult, based on the creator god Makemake, who had previously been just one of Easter's pantheon of gods. The cult was centered at Orongo village on the rim of Rano Kau caldera, overlooking the three largest offshore islets to which nesting seabirds had become confined. The new religion developed its own new art styles, expressed especially in petroglyphs (rock carvings) of women's genitals, birdmen, and birds (in order of decreasing frequency), carved not only on Orongo monuments but also on toppled *moai* and *pukao* elsewhere. Each year the Orongo cult organized a competition between men to swim across the cold, shark-infested, one-mile-wide strait separating the islets from Easter itself, to collect the first egg laid in that season by Sooty Terns, to swim back to Easter with the unbroken egg, and to be anointed 'Birdman of the year' for the following year. The last Orongo ceremony took place in 1867 and was witnessed by Catholic missionaries, just as the residue of Easter Island society not already destroyed by the islanders themselves was being destroyed by the outside world.

Europeans and explanations

The sad story of European impacts on Easter Islanders may be quickly summarized. After Captain Cook's brief sojourn in 1774, there was a steady trickle of European visitors. As documented for Hawaii, Fiji, and many other Pacific islands, they must be assumed to have introduced European diseases and thereby to have killed many previously unexposed islanders, though our first specific mention of such an epidemic is of smallpox around 1836. Again as on other Pacific islands, 'black-birding,' the kidnapping of islanders to become slaves, began on Easter around 1805 and climaxed in 1862–63, the grimmest year of Easter's history, when two dozen Peruvian ships abducted about 1,500 people (half of the surviving population) and sold them at auction to work in Peru's guano mines and other menial jobs. Most of those kidnapped died in captivity. Under international pressure, Peru repatriated a dozen surviving captives, who brought another smallpox epidemic to the island. Catholic missionaries took up residence in 1864. By 1872 there were only 111 islanders left on Easter.

European traders introduced sheep to Easter in the 1870s and claimed land ownership. In 1888 the Chilean government annexed Easter, which effectively became a sheep ranch managed by a Chile-based Scottish company. All islanders were confined to living in one village and to working for the company, being paid in goods at the company store rather than in cash. A revolt by the islanders in 1914 was ended by the arrival of a Chilean warship. Grazing by the company's sheep, goats, and horses caused soil erosion and eliminated most of what had remained of the native vegetation, including the last surviving hauhau and toromiro individuals on Easter around 1934. Not until 1966 did islanders become Chilean citizens. Today, islanders are undergoing a resurgence of cultural pride, and the economy is being stimulated by the arrival of several airplane flights each week from Santiago and Tahiti by Chile's national airline, carrying visitors (like Barry Rolett and me) attracted by the famous statues. However, even a brief visit makes obvious that tensions remain between islanders and mainland-born Chileans, who are now represented in roughly equal numbers on Easter.

Easter Island's famous rongo-rongo writing system was undoubtedly invented by the islanders, but there is no evidence for its existence until its first mention by the resident Catholic missionary in 1864. All 25 surviving objects with writing appear to postdate European contact; some of them are pieces of foreign wood or a European oar, and some may have been manufactured by islanders specifically to sell to representatives of Tahiti's Catholic bishop, who became interested in the writing and sought examples. In 1995 linguist Steven Fischer announced a decipherment of rongo-rongo texts as procreation chants, but his interpretation is

debated by other scholars. Most Easter Island specialists, including Fischer, now conclude that the invention
of rongo-rongo was inspired by the islanders' first contact with writing during the Spanish landing of 1770,
or else by the trauma of the 1862–63 Peruvian slave raid
that killed so many carriers of oral knowledge.

In part because of this history of exploitation and
oppression, there has been resistance among both
islanders and scholars to acknowledging the reality
of self-inflicted environmental damage before Roggeveen's arrival in 1722, despite all the detailed
evidence that I have summarized. In essence, the
islanders are saying, 'Our ancestors would never have
done that,' while visiting scientists are saying, 'Those
nice people whom we have come to love would never
have done that.' For example, Michel Orliac wrote
about similar questions of environmental change in
Tahiti, '. . . it is at least as likely – if not more so – that
environmental modifications originated in natural
causes rather than in human activities. This is a
much-debated question (McFadgen 1985; Grant 1985;
McGlone 1989) to which I do not claim to bring a
definitive solution, even if my affection for the Polynesians incites me to choose natural actions [e.g., cyclones]
to explain the damages suffered by the environment.'
Three specific objections or alternative theories have
been raised.

First, it has been suggested that Easter's deforested condition seen by Roggeveen in 1722 was not caused by the islanders in isolation but resulted in some unspecified way from disruption caused by unrecorded European visitors before Roggeveen. It is perfectly possible that there were indeed one or more such unrecorded visits: many Spanish galleons were sailing across the Pacific in the 1500s and 1600s, and the islanders' nonchalant, unafraid, curious reaction to Roggeveen does suggest prior experience of Europeans, rather than the shocked reaction expected for people who had been living in total isolation and had assumed themselves to be the only humans in the world. However, we have no specific knowledge of any pre-1722 visit, nor is it obvious how it would have triggered deforestation. Even before Magellan became the first European to cross the Pacific in 1521, abundant evidence attests to massive human impacts on Easter: extinctions of all the land bird species, disappearance of porpoises and tuna from the diet, declines of forest tree pollen in Flenley's sediment cores before 1300, deforestation of the Poike Peninsula by around 1400, lack of radiocarbon-dated palm nuts after 1500, and so on.

A second objection is that deforestation might instead have been due to natural climate changes, such as droughts or El Niño episodes. It would not surprise me at all if a contributing role of climate change does eventually emerge for Easter, because we shall see that climatic downturns did. At present, we lack information about climate changes on Easter in the relevant period of A.D. 900–1700: we don't know whether the climate got drier and stormier and less favorable to forest survival (as postulated by critics), or wetter and less stormy and more favorable to forest survival. But there seems to me to be compelling evidence against climate change by itself having caused the deforestation and bird extinctions: the palm trunk casts in Mt. Terevaka's lava flows prove that the giant palm had already survived on Easter for several hundred thousand years; and Flenley's sediment cores demonstrate pollen of the palm, tree daisies, toromiro, and half-a-dozen other tree species on Easter between 38,000 and 21,000 years ago. Hence Easter's plants had already survived innumerable droughts and El Niño events, making it unlikely that all those native tree species finally chose a time coincidentally just after the arrival of those innocent humans to drop dead simultaneously in response to yet another drought or El Niño event. In fact, Flenley's records show that a cool dry period on Easter between 26,000 and 12,000 years ago, more severe than any worldwide cool dry period in the last thousand years, merely caused Easter's trees at higher elevation to undergo a retreat to the lowlands, from which they subsequently recovered.

A third objection is that Easter Islanders surely wouldn't have been so foolish as to cut down all their trees, when the consequences would have been so obvious to them. As Catherine Orliac expressed it, 'Why destroy a forest that one needs for his [i.e., the Easter Islanders'] material and spiritual survival?' This is indeed a key question, one that has nagged not only Catherine Orliac but also my University of California students, me, and everyone else who has wondered about self-inflicted environmental damage. I have often asked myself, 'What did the Easter Islander who cut down the last palm tree say while he was doing it?' Like modern loggers, did he shout 'Jobs, not trees!'? Or: 'Technology will solve our problems, never fear, we'll find a substitute for wood'? Or: 'We don't have proof that there aren't palms somewhere else on Easter, we need more research, your proposed ban on logging is premature and driven by fear-mongering'? Similar questions arise for every society that has inadvertently damaged its environment. Societies nevertheless do make such mistakes.

Why was Easter fragile

We still have not faced the question why Easter Island ranks as such an extreme example of deforestation.

After all, the Pacific encompasses thousands of inhabited islands, almost all of whose inhabitants were chopping down trees, clearing gardens, burning firewood, building canoes, and using wood and rope for houses and other things. Yet, among all those islands, only three in the Hawaiian Archipelago, all of them much drier than Easter – the two islets of Necker and Nihoa, and the larger island of Niihau – even approach Easter in degree of deforestation. Nihoa still supports one species of large palm tree, and it is uncertain whether tiny Necker, with an area of barely forty acres, ever had trees. Why were Easter Islanders unique, or nearly so, in destroying every tree? The answer sometimes given, 'because Easter's palm and toromiro were very slow-growing,' fails to explain why at least 19 other tree or plant species related to or the same as species still widespread on East Polynesian islands were eliminated on Easter but not on other islands. I suspect that this question lies behind the reluctance of Easter Islanders themselves and of some scientists to accept that the islanders caused the deforestation, because that conclusion seems to imply that they were uniquely bad or improvident among Pacific peoples.

Barry Rolett and I were puzzled by that apparent uniqueness of Easter. Actually, it's just part of a broader puzzling question: why degree of deforestation varies among Pacific islands in general. For example, Mangareva, most of the Cook and Austral Islands, and the leeward sides of the main Hawaiian and Fijian Islands were largely deforested, though not completely as in the case of Easter. The Societies and Marquesas, and the windward sides of the main Hawaiian and Fijian Islands, supported primary forests at higher elevation and a mixture of secondary forests, fernlands, and grasslands at low elevation. Tonga, Samoa, most of the Bismarcks and Solomons, and Makatea (the largest of the Tuamotus) remained largely forested. How can all that variation be explained?

Barry began by combing through the journals of early European explorers of the Pacific, to locate descriptions of what the islands looked like then. That enabled him to extract the degree of deforestation on 81 islands as first seen by Europeans – i.e., after centuries or millennia of impacts by native Pacific Islanders but before European impacts. For those same 81 islands, we then tabulated values of nine physical factors whose interisland variation we thought might contribute to explaining those different outcomes of deforestation. Some trends immediately became obvious to us when we just eyeballed the data, but we ground the data through many statistical analyses in order to be able to put numbers on the trends.

What Affects Deforestation on Pacific Islands?

Deforestation is more severe on:
   dry islands than wet islands;
   cold high-latitude islands than warm equatorial
      islands;
   old volcanic islands than young volcanic islands;
   islands without aerial ash fallout than islands with it;
   islands far from Central Asia's dust plume than
      islands near it;
   islands without *makatea* rock than islands with it;
   low islands than high islands;
   remote islands than islands with near neighbors; and
   small islands than big islands.

It turned out that all nine of the physical variables did contribute to the outcome (see the list above). Most important were variations in rainfall and latitude: dry islands, and cooler islands farther from the equator (at higher latitude), ended up more deforested than did wetter equatorial islands. That was as we had expected: the rate of plant growth and of seedling establishment increases with rainfall and with temperature. When one chops trees down in a wet hot place like the New Guinea lowlands, within a year new trees 20 feet tall have sprung up on the site, but tree growth is much slower in a cold dry desert. Hence regrowth can keep pace with moderate rates of cutting trees on wet hot islands, leaving the island in a steady state of being largely tree-covered.

Three other variables – island age, ash fallout, and dust fallout – had effects that we hadn't anticipated, because we hadn't been familiar with the scientific literature on the maintenance of soil fertility. Old islands that hadn't experienced any volcanic activity for over a million years ended up more deforested than young, recently active volcanic islands. That's because soil derived from fresh lava and ash contains nutrients that are necessary for plant growth, and that gradually become leached out by rain on older islands. One of the two main ways that those nutrients then become renewed on Pacific islands is by fallout of ash carried in the air from volcanic explosions. But the Pacific Ocean is divided by a line famous to geologists and known as the Andesite Line. In the Southwest Pacific on the Asian side of that line, volcanoes blow out ash that may be wind-carried for hundreds of miles and that maintains the fertility even of islands (like New Caledonia) that have no volcanoes of their own. In the central and eastern Pacific beyond the Andesite Line, the main aerial input of nutrients to renew soil fertility is instead in dust carried high in the atmosphere by winds from the steppes of Central

Asia. Hence islands east of the Andesite Line, and far from Asia's dust plume, ended up more deforested than islands within the Andesite Line or nearer to Asia.

Another variable required consideration only for half a dozen islands that consist of the rock known as makatea – basically, a coral reef thrust into the air by geological uplift. The name arises from the Tuamotu island of Makatea, which consists largely of that rock. Makatea terrain is absolute hell to walk over; the deeply fissured, razor-sharp coral cuts one's boots, feet, and hands to shreds. When I first encountered makatea on Rennell Island in the Solomons, it took me 10 minutes to walk a hundred yards, and I was in constant terror of lacerating my hands on a coral boulder if I touched it while thoughtlessly extending my hands to maintain my balance. Makatea can slice up stout modern boots within a few days of walking. While Pacific Islanders somehow managed to get around on it in bare feet, even they had problems. No one who has endured the agony of walking on makatea will be surprised that Pacific islands with makatea ended up less deforested than those without it.

That leaves three variables with more complex effects: elevation, distance, and area. High islands tended to become less deforested (even in their lowlands) than low islands, because mountains generate clouds and rain, which descends to the lowlands as streams, stimulating lowland plant growth by their water, by their transport of eroded nutrients, and by transport of atmospheric dust. The mountains themselves may remain forest-covered if they are too high or too steep for gardening. Remote islands became more deforested than islands with near neighbors – possibly because islanders were more likely to stay home and do things impacting their own environment than to spend time and energy visiting other islands to trade, raid, or settle. Big islands tended to become less deforested than small islands, for numerous reasons including lower perimeter/area ratios, hence fewer marine resources per person and lower population densities, more centuries required to chop down the forest, and more areas unsuitable for gardening remaining.

How does Easter rate according to these nine variables predisposing to deforestation? It has the third highest latitude, among the lowest rainfalls, the lowest volcanic ash fallout, the lowest Asian dust fallout, no makatea, and the second greatest distance from neighboring islands. It is among the lower and smaller of the 81 islands that Barry Rolett and I studied. All eight of those variables make Easter susceptible to deforestation. Easter's volcanoes are of moderate age (probably 200,000 to 600,000 years); Easter's Poike

Peninsula, its oldest volcano, was the first part of Easter to become deforested and exhibits the worst soil erosion today. Combining the effects of all those variables, Barry's and my statistical model predicted that Easter, Nihoa, and Necker should be the worst deforested Pacific islands. That agrees with what actually happened: Nihoa and Necker ended up with no human left alive and with only one tree species standing (Nihoa's palm), while Easter ended up with no tree species standing and with about 90% of its former population gone.

In short, the reason for Easter's unusually severe degree of deforestation isn't that those seemingly nice people really were unusually bad or improvident. Instead, they had the misfortune to be living in one of the most fragile environments, at the highest risk for deforestation, of any Pacific people. For Easter Island, we can specify in detail the factors underlying environmental fragility.

Easter as metaphor

Easter's isolation makes it the clearest example of a society that destroyed itself by overexploiting its own resources. Of the checklist of factors to be considered in connection with environmental collapses, two of those factors – attacks by neighboring enemy societies, and loss of support from neighboring friendly societies – played no role in Easter's collapse, because there is no evidence that there were any enemies or friends in contact with Easter Island society after its founding. Even if it turns out that some canoes did arrive subsequently, such contacts could not have been on a large enough scale to constitute either dangerous attacks or important support. For a role of a third factor, climate change, we also have no evidence at present, though it may emerge in the future. That leaves us with just two main sets of factors behind Easter's collapse: human environmental impacts, especially deforestation and destruction of bird populations; and the political, social, and religious factors behind the impacts, such as the impossibility of emigration as an escape valve because of Easter's isolation, a focus on statue construction for reasons already discussed, and competition between clans and chiefs driving the erection of bigger statues requiring more wood, rope, and food.

The Easter Islanders' isolation probably also explains why I have found that their collapse, more than the collapse of any other pre-industrial society, haunts my readers and students. The parallels between Easter Island and the whole modern world are chillingly obvious. Thanks to globalization, international trade, jet planes, and the Internet, all countries on Earth today share resources and affect each other, just as did Easter's dozen clans. Polynesian Easter Island was as isolated in the Pacific Ocean as the Earth is today in space. When the Easter Islanders got into difficulties, there was nowhere to which they could flee, nor to which they could turn for help; nor shall we modern Earthlings have recourse elsewhere if our troubles increase. Those are the reasons why people see the collapse of Easter Island society as a metaphor, a worst-case scenario, for what may lie ahead of us in our own future.

Of course, the metaphor is imperfect. Our situation today differs in important respects from that of Easter Islanders in the 17th century. Some of those differences increase the danger for us: for instance, if mere thousands of Easter Islanders with just stone tools and their own muscle power sufficed to destroy their environment and thereby destroyed their society, how can billions of people with metal tools and machine power now fail to do worse?

Further Reading

The general reader seeking an overview of Easter Island should begin with three books: John Flenley and Paul Bahn, *The Enigmas of Easter Island* (New York: Oxford University Press, 2003), updating Paul Bahn and John Flenley, *Easter Island, Earth Island* (London: Thames and Hudson, 1992); Jo Anne Van Tilburg, *Easter Island: Archaeology, Ecology, and Culture* (Washington, D.C.: Smithsonian Institution Press, 1994); and Jo Anne Van Tilburg, *Among Stone Giants* (New York: Scribner, 2003). The last-mentioned book is a biography of Katherine Routledge, a remarkable English archeologist whose 1914–15 visit enabled her to interview islanders with personal memories of the last Orongo ceremonies, and whose life was as colorful as a fantastic novel.

Two other recent books are Catherine and Michel Orliac, *The Silent Gods: Mysteries of Easter Island* (London: Thames and Hudson, 1995), a short illustrated overview; and John Loret and John Tancredi, eds., *Easter Island: Scientific Exploration into the World's Environmental Problems in Microcosm* (New York: Kluwer/

Plenum, 2003), 13 chapters on results of recent exped-itions. Anyone who becomes seriously interested in Easter Island will want to read two classic earlier books: Katherine Routledge's own account, *The Mystery of Easter Island* (London: Sifton Praed, 1919, reprinted by Adventure Unlimited Press, Kempton, Ill., 1998), and Alfred Métraux, *Ethnology of Easter Island* (Honolulu: Bishop Museum Bulletin 160, 1940, reprinted 1971). Eric Kjellgren, ed., *Splendid Isolation: Art of Easter Island* (New York: Metropolitan Museum of Art, 2001) assem-bles dozens of photos, many in color, of petroglyphs, rongo-rongo boards, *moai kavakava*, barkcloth figures, and a red feather headdress of a type that may have inspired the red stone *pukao*.

Articles by Jo Anne Van Tilburg include 'Easter Island (Rapa Nui) archaeology since 1955: some thoughts on progress, problems and potential,' pp. 555–577 in J. M. Davidson et al., eds., *Oceanic Culture History: Essays in Honour of Roger Green* (New Zealand Journal of Archaeology Special Publication, 1996); Jo Anne Van Tilburg and Cristián Arévalo Pakarati, 'The Rapanui carvers' perspective: notes and obser-vations on the experimental replication of monolithic sculpture (*moai*),' pp. 280–290 in A. Herle et al., eds., *Pacific Art: Persistence, Change and Meaning* (Bathurst, Australia: Crawford House, 2002); and Jo Anne Van Tilburg and Ted Ralston, 'Megaliths and mariners:

experimental archaeology on Easter Island (Rapa Nui),' in press in K. L. Johnson, ed., *Onward and Upward! Papers in Honor of Clement W. Meighan* (University Press of America). The latter two of those three articles describe experimental studies aimed at understanding how many people were required to carve and transport statues, and how long it would have taken.

Many good books accessible to the general reader describe the settlement of Polynesia or the Pacific as a whole. They include Patrick Kirch, *On the Road of the Winds: An Archaeological History of the Pacific Islands Before European Contact* (Berkeley: University of California Press, 2000), *The Lapita Peoples: Ancestors of the Oceanic World* (Oxford: Blackwell, 1997), and *The Evolution of the Polynesian Chiefdoms* (Cambridge: Cambridge University Press, 1984); Peter Bellwood, *The Polynesians: Prehistory of an Island People,* revised edition (London: Thames and Hudson, 1987); and Geoffrey Irwin, *The Prehistoric Exploration and Colonisation of the Pacific* (Cambridge: Cambridge University Press, 1992). David Lewis, *We, the Navigators* (Honolulu: University Press of Hawaii, 1972) is a unique account of traditional Pacific navigational techniques, by a modern sailor who studied those techniques by embarking on long voyages with surviving traditional navigators. Patrick Kirch and Terry Hunt, eds., *Historical Ecology in the Pacific Islands:*

Prehistoric Environmental and Landscape Change (New Haven, Conn.: Yale University Press, 1997) consists of papers about human environmental impacts on Pacific Islands other than Easter.

Two books by Thor Heyerdahl that inspired my interest and that of many others in Easter Island are *The Kon-Tiki Expedition* (London: Allen & Unwin, 1950) and *Aku-Aku: The Secret of Easter Island* (London: Allen & Unwin, 1958). A rather different interpretation emerges from the excavations of the archeologists whom Heyerdahl brought to Easter Island, as described in Thor Heyerdahl and E. Ferdon, Jr., eds., *Reports of the Norwegian Archaeological Expedition to Easter Island and the East Pacific, vol. 1: The Archaeology of Easter Island* (London: Allen & Unwin, 1961). Steven Fischer, *Glyph Breaker* (New York: Copernicus, 1997) and *Rongorongo: The Easter Island Script* (Oxford: Oxford University Press, 1997) describe Fischer's efforts at deciphering the Rongo-rongo text. Andrew Sharp, ed., *The Journal of Jacob Roggeveen* (London: Oxford University Press, 1970) reprints on pp. 89–106 the first European eyewitness description of Easter Island.

An archeological mapping of Easter Island is summarized in Claudio Cristino, Patricia Vargas, and R. Izaurieta, *Atlas Arqueológico de Isla de Pascua* (Santiago: University of Chile, 1981). Detailed articles about Easter Island are published regularly in the *Rapa Nui Journal* by the Easter Island Foundation, which also publishes occasional conferences about the island. Important collections of papers are Claudio Cristino, Patricia Vargas et al., eds., *First International Congress, Easter Island and East Polynesia, vol. 1 Archaeology* (Santiago: University of Chile, 1988); Patricia Vargas Casanova, ed., *Easter Island and East Polynesia Prehistory* (Santiago: University of Chile, 1998); and Christopher Stevenson and William Ayres, eds., *Easter Island Archaeology: Research on Early Rapanui Culture* (Los Osos, Calif.: Easter Island Foundation, 2000). A summary of the history of cultural contacts is to be found in Claudio Cristino et al., *Isla de Pascua: Procesos, Alcances y Efectos de la Aculturación* (Easter Island: University of Chile, 1984).

David Steadman reports his identification of bird bones and other remains excavated at Anakena Beach in three papers: 'Extinctions of birds in Eastern Polynesia: a review of the record, and comparisons with other Pacific Island groups' (*Journal of Archaeological Science* 16:177–205 (1989)), and 'Stratigraphy, chronology, and cultural context of an early faunal assemblage from Easter Island' (*Asian Perspectives* 33:79–96 (1994)), both with Patricia Vargas and Claudio Cristino; and 'Prehistoric extinctions of Pacific Island birds: biodiversity meets zooarchaeology' (*Science* 267:1123–1131 (1995)). William Ayres, 'Easter Island subsistence' (*Journal de la Société des Océanistes* 80:103–124 (1985)) provides further archaeological evidence of foods consumed. For solution of the mystery of the Easter Island palm and other insights from pollen in sediment cores, see J. R. Flenley and Sarah King, 'Late Quaternary pollen records from Easter Island' (*Nature* 307:47–50 (1984)), J. Dransfield et al., 'A recently extinct palm from Easter Island' (*Nature* 312:750–752 (1984)), and J. R. Flenley et al., 'The Late Quaternary vegetational and climatic history of Easter Island' (*Journal of Quaternary Science* 6:85–115 (1991)). Catherine Orliac's identifications are reported in a paper in the above-cited edited volume by Stevenson and Ayres, and in 'Données nouvelles sur la composition de la flore de l'Île de Pâques' (*Journal de la Société des Océanistes* 2:23–31 (1998)). Among the papers resulting from the archeological surveys by Claudio Cristino and his colleagues are Christopher Stevenson and Claudio Cristino, 'Residential settlement history of the Rapa Nui coastal plain' (*Journal of New World Archaeology* 7:29–38 (1986)); Daris Swindler, Andrea Drusini, and Claudio Cristino, 'Variation and frequency of three-rooted first permanent molars in precontact Easter Islanders: anthropological significance' (*Journal of the Polynesian Society* 106:175–183 (1997)); and Claudio Cristino and Patricia Vargas, 'Ahu Tongariki, Easter Island: chronological and sociopolitical significance' (*Rapa Nui Journal* 13:67–69 (1999)).

Christopher Stevenson's papers on intensive agriculture and lithic mulches include *Archaeological Investigations on Easter Island; Maunga Tari: an Upland Agriculture Complex* (Los Osos, Calif.: Easter Island Foundation, 1995), (with Joan Wozniak and Sonia Haoa) 'Prehistoric agriculture production on Easter Island (Rapa Nui), Chile' (*Antiquity* 73:801–812 (1999)), and (with Thegn Ladefoged and Sonia Haoa) 'Productive strategies in an uncertain environment: prehistoric agriculture on Easter Island' (*Rapa Nui Journal* 16:17–22 (2002)). Christopher Stevenson, 'Territorial divisions on Easter Island in the 16th century: evidence from the distribution of ceremonial architecture,' pp. 213–229 in T. Ladefoged and M. Graves, eds., *Pacific Landscapes* (Los Osos, Calif.: Easter Island Foundation, 2002) reconstructs the boundaries of Easter's 11 traditional clans.

Dale Lightfoot, 'Morphology and ecology of lithic-mulch agriculture' (*Geographical Review* 84:172–185 (1994)) and Carleton White et al., 'Water conservation through an Anasazi gardening technique' (*New Mexico Journal of Science* 38:251–278 (1998)) provide evidence for the function of lithic mulches elsewhere in the world. Andreas Mieth and Hans-Rudolf Bork 'Diminution and degradation of environmental resources by prehistoric land use on Poike Peninsula, Easter Island (Rapa Nui)' (*Rapa Nui Journal* 17:34–41 (2003)) discuss deforestation and erosion on the Poike Peninsula.

Karsten Haase et al., 'The petrogenetic evolution of lavas from Easter Island and neighboring seamounts, near-ridge hotspot volcanoes in the S.E. Pacific' (*Journal of Petrology* 38:785–813 (1997)) analyze the dates and chemical compositions of Easter's volcanoes. Erika Hagelberg et al., 'DNA from ancient Easter Islanders' (*Nature* 369:25–26 (1994)) analyze DNA extracted from 12 Easter Island skeletons. James Brander and M. Scott Taylor, 'The simple economics of Easter Island: a Ricardo-Malthus model of renewable resource use' (*American Economic Review* 38: 119–138 (1998)) give an economist's view of overexploitation on Easter.